Our family started back in the early 1940s. Jeremy Elliott Applegate was born Paul Andrew Boyce in San Jose California. Jeremy was the youngest child in the family and my brother David was the oldest. David was born in 1943 and Jeremy in 1965, so we covered a wide range of ages. There were eleven kids in our family. Jeremy left home at a young age and lived with other family members off-and-on until finally he went missing for sixteen years. We never saw him again. We all thought he was working and making it big in Hollywood. I did not hear about his death until the time my mother was dying, when a family member looked Jeremy up on a website and we learned of his suicide. I was totally devastated; it was like a bad dream and I just wanted to wake up and find out it wasn't true.

Jeremy always wanted to be an actor. He appeared in numerous television shows and movies — but just small parts. His biggest break was in the movie "Heathers," in which he played the part of an editor working on the school paper.

He never really made it big. Most days he was depressed, and he frequently failed to show up for auditions. As part of his therapy, the doctors told him to avoid contact with his family. The medications he was taking made him paranoid. Jeremy was in and out of mental hospitals for years. We are still trying to find out the details of his medical troubles.

I decided to write this book as a memorial to my beloved brother. To show Jeremy how much I loved him, how much I miss him — and how much I wish I could have been a bigger part of his life.

— Margaret J. Gomez

Jeremy

Memories of an Actor

✦

A Biography of Jeremy Elliott Applegate

By his sister

Peggy J. Gomez

If tears could build a stairway
And memories were a lane
We would walk right up to Heaven
And bring you back again.

No farewell words were spoken,
No time to say goodbye;
You were gone before we knew it —
And only you know why.

Our hearts still ache in sadness,
And secret tears still flow.
What it meant to lose you
No one will ever know.

But now we know you want us
To mourn for you no more;
To remember all our happy times
Life still has more in store.

Since you'll never be forgotten
We hold for you today
A hallowed happy place
Within our hearts
Is where you'll always stay.

— Jennifer Johann

CHAPTER ONE

CHILDHOOD

Jeremy Applegate's birth name was Paul Andrew Boyce. He was born August 29, 1965 in San Jose, California, and was named after Paul McCartney. He was the last-born child in a family with five brothers and four sisters. Paul was born with the bilabial cord wrapped around is neck — and he could easily have died. He had blond hair and blue eyes. He was a beautiful baby; but our mother did not want another child. Mother didn't care for or want children. Back in those days birth control was unheard of. Mother bore a child every two years, so she must have been pregnant thirteen times.

When Paul was brought home from the hospital, it was up to his brothers and sisters to care for him. As a baby, Mother would leave him alone for hours crying. I couldn't stand it ... so every night one of us would sneak in his room and bring him to sleep with us. Mother would scream, "Get the baby down here now!" No one wanted to answer her, we were afraid.

Then the next day, we would have to go to school — and we hated to leave Paul with our mother. She frequently left little Paul alone many times during the day. Once, my oldest brother David had a job interview, so he took Paul with him. We all took turns taking care of the baby wherever we could — except when we were in school and couldn't take Paul with us.

When I would come home from school, Paul would still be in his crib screaming and sobbing, sopping wet and lying in a soaked sheet. I don't remember that our mother ever changed his diapers. God but we just hated the way she treated Paul! That poor baby would bang his head on the crib so hard that bars were coming loose. Mother would yell, "Paul stop that!" We would find bruises and red marks on his body as well as very bad diaper rash. This went on for years until he was able to walk.

* * *

One day when I came home from school calling for Paul, he was nowhere in sight. I was terribly worried because I couldn't find him anywhere. So I went looking from room to room — until I finally found him sleeping under my sister's beds. He was terrified of Mother and had been hiding there under the bed until he fell asleep. One day, I saw Mother slap Paul terribly hard, but he did not cry. So she just kept slapping him on the face. She said, "Why don't you cry, Paul? — you must like being slapped ..."

But he would not cry. His face was so red that she left her hand marks on his face from slapping so hard. She raised her hand to slap him again, but my sister Rosemary blocked her hand and said, "Stop it — he's just a baby!" Mother turned to my sister with that devil look in her eyes, raised her foot and kicked Rosemary in the crotch, bringing her to her knees. It was so painful that I had to help Rosemary stand up.

Mother even made Paul save his urine in large glass containers in his closet. We never knew what that was all about.

My brothers and I had to do all the grocery shopping. We took Paul with us to protect him and try to keep him safe.

Mother would talk to herself and then answer back too — just as if there was someone else in the room. She never wanted Paul. Mother told everyone that he was an accident, a change of a life child. Paul needed a real Mother; he needed love. He needed clothing and food that was not rotten and discarded. Paul never had what a normal family should have provided. None of us ever had those things. My brothers and sisters tried their best, but we were just kids ourselves. It was as if we were trying to be adults but were trapped in children's bodies — and fighting so hard to get out. All of us kids took turned dressing Paul and buying clothes for him.

In the summertime, we would take Paul to the beach. He would go everywhere with us as if he was our own child. When my

Paul's childhood home.

brother and I took him visiting to friends, they thought he was my son.

* * *

My father is a kind and gentle man; he never knew that Paul was being abused. He did what he could to provide for his family. Dad worked two jobs six days a week. He earned a fair amount, but Mother hid the money she should have been spending on us. Dad once bought Paul a great toy — a battery-operated car, which in the 1960's was the latest thing. Paul had fun riding that around the house.

When Paul was two, brother David took him to the zoo cared for him as he was his own child. David took him to the Santa Cruz board walk to play on the rides. It was the closest Pacific ocean park. He had fun listening to the bands play there music on the beach. David took him to see the a dinosaur rise out in and out of the water, it turned to the right while growling, then it went back down under the water. Paul watched for hours with his brother David. He loved the beach and went there often.

Whenever Paul had company, Mother would put on her phony face and act as if she was a great mom. Soon as his friends left, she would begin slapping him around and calling him terrible names you should never say to an adult, much less a child. He was only three years old.

* * *

In 1968 when I was eighteen, Paul was to be the ring-bearer at my wedding, but he was so terrified he couldn't do it. After I moved out of the house, Mother would frequently drop Paul off to stay with me. I didn't know why; I guess she didn't want to deal with him. So I potty-trained him and tried to help him as much as I could. When it came time for Mother to pick him up again, he would scream and say, "Please — I want to stay! Don't make me go with her ..."

It tore me up inside to see him go. If I'd had my way, I would never have let him go. If only things had been different maybe he might have been able to lead a normal life. What is a normal life? We all never had that. Paul was a child born to a sick sociopath we all had to call Mother.

When Paul was four, he had hours of fun with brother Richard, who took him to picnics and amusements park rides. Paul had fun going on to high school outings with his brother. Richard showed off Paul to his high school sweetheart. When they went on hay rides, friends would ask Richard if Paul was his own son. Maybe it was because they looked so much alike and got along so well together.

* * *

As he grew older, Paul began abusing the family pets — which is a typical response from a child who has been abused himself. There we cats everywhere in the house. Once Paul grabbed a few kittens put them in kitchen canisters filled with sugar-water and left them in there until they were dead. When Paul was about five years old, his older brother Brian took him to the railroad track, where he tired his Diaper Dan doll to the tracks.

Another time, Paul was playing with his older brother Brian. Paul was chasing Brian, and as they passed through the kitchen, Paul picked up a butcher knife. He ran after Brian with the knife, waving it in the air and cutting Brian's shirt — but the knife never broke the skin.

CHAPTER TWO

JOEY

Paul had a made-up imaginary friend he called him Joey. He would talk to him for hours. I guess that was the only outlet he had to escape his own abusive life. Whenever Paul would play house, he would set another place for Joey. He made up a dummy and dressed him in his own clothes. It was as if he was acting out his own movie.

* * *

Brother Dennis loved Paul like his own son. They went on a lot of fishing trips to the Santa Cruz River. Dennis took him on his first visit to the San Francisco Zoo. In that year is when the zoo started charging for admission which was one dollar. Dennis spent hours with Paul looking at all the exotic animals. They had a lot fun that day. Paul loved it and wanted to visit again.

* * *

Paul was very intelligent for his age. The teachers at his school couldn't believe how bright he was for seven-years-old. He once made an anatomically-correct model of his body out of playdough, moulding the outside first and then opening it up to make all the internal organs too.

He would stay over every weekend at the house of one of his brothers or sisters. He loved to visit us because he would be very well cared for. He had someone else to play with besides just himself. When Mother came to pick him up, he would hide because he didn't want to go. He would cry and go into a rage. He would grab a hold of my leg and would not let go. He was getting into the car screaming, "Please help me I do not want to go home" there was nothing I could do.

Once when Paul was about eight years old, I found him in the living room with a rope around his neck and choking. I was so shocked I screamed, "What have you done? Oh my god!" as I untangled the rope from his throat

Was this an accident? — or did he want to die even then?

If I had not been at home, he would have died.

* * *

Rosemary often took Paul shopping dressed him in the best clothes. They spent time at the park playing ball, throwing a Frisbee around, or flying kites. Rosemary is the sister who named Paul after one of the Beatles.

Paul made his own homemade clay-mation movie at the age of ten using an old movie projector. Joey was the star of the movie. Paul would move Joey every few inches and take a picture, and move his arms and legs as if he was real person. He did this though-out the whole movie. At the end, Joey was destroyed — blown up into a million pieces.

I had that movie he made, but Mother threw it out.

Paul was so creative. He was always role-playing, and we all thought he was meant to be an actor.

Sister Marian played board games with Paul and took him on airplane rides. Marian baked him his favorite cookies — which were chocolate chip and peanut butter. Paul spent every other weekend with Marian having the best time ever.

When Paul was twelve, brother Philip played football with him, took him to the beach, taught and him to ride his first bike. They had so much fun together they did not want the days to end. Some times Paul would spend the night at Philip's house.

Brother Brian was eight years older than Paul. They spent a lot of time together doing guy things. Some of it good some not. Paul tagged along with Brian where-ever he went.

CHAPTER THREE

ALWAYS HUNGRY

Paul didn't have much to eat as a child. His bedroom was like a pigsty, and there was mold in the refrigerator covering the food like a blanket. The stench was terrible; Mother never cleaned it, it made your stomach upset. Poor Paul would say, "Please can you get some food in this house?" — and she would reply, "The food is still good, just wash it off." She didn't care if he got sick. Paul would use her charge card to order pizza. Mother would not find out until later when she got the bill in the mail. He would steal money out of her purse for food.

* * *

One day the school nurse phoned because Paul had passed out. Mother showed up at the nurse's office just as the nurse was giving him smelling salts. "Oh, Paul!" she said. "What happened, Sweetie?"

Paul just gave her a dirty look.

As they were walking to the car, Mother said, "You fool! What the Hell is wrong with you? I don't want anyone to know what goes on in our household."

Paul was very depressed; he had hoped that someone would find out about his home life so that he would not have live with her anymore. Mother went wild with rage because she'd had to pick him up from school. She told him to clean up the house.

He was still terribly hungry, for he had not eaten since the previous night. How could he get something to eat without her seeing him?

Paul called me at home, and I picked him up at the corner. He was crying. "I hate Mother! I'm so hungry, I'm feeling sick ..." So I fixed him a sandwich and a bowl of chicken noodle soup, which he wolfed down because he was starving. Poor Paul — I wanted so badly to keep him with me.

I took care of Paul like he was my own child. Paul was only four years older than my son John, and they grew up together. They spent hours together riding bikes, swimming, and role-playing. We spent a lot of time making Christmas ornaments out of play dough. After the ornaments were baked Paul and my son would paint them. Then get them ready to hang on the tree.

Paul made Christmas ornaments from playdough. He was very much into detail, and once made a model of Santa Claus. Paul was meticulous — he insisted that it have the right colors, the correct size, and precise shape.

By this time, Paul was the only one left home with Mother. My brothers and sisters all felt very sorry for him, and would bake Paul cookies and real home-cooked meals.

CHAPTER FOUR

ILLNESS

Paul had very bad allergies complicated with asthma due to the stress he was under, and to the filth of the house he was living in. He frequently had to be taken to the hospital emergency room because of his asthma attacks. Paul was there so often that Dad rented a nebulizer machine for him so he could breathe.

My brother's dream was to have a mother who loved him and would take care of him; the dream of having a normal family life. However we all knew that was just a dream and would never happen. Paul's heath always improved whenever he was not at home — when he was happy.

Many of us in the family had illness as children from lack of food and improper care. Some of my siblings had arthritis so crippling that they used crutches. Others had nosebleeds from poor eating and lack of proper food.

Sometimes all Paul could find in the house was milk, and he would drink that until he was full. Back in the 1960's, milk was delivered to your door in glass bottles — so Paul would order extra things from the milkman, such as orange juice, chocolate milk, cottage cheese, and popsicles. That was one way of getting enough to eat. Paul was very clever about getting food — until he was caught by Mother. Then he would start using her credit card to make phone orders so he could eat. He ordered more pizzas, fast foods, or anything he could in order to eat.

* * *

One time when Paul was having a severe asthma attack, Mother said, "Get out of here. I never wanted you anyway ..." So he called my sister Rosemary, who took him to the hospital. It was an especially bad attack this time, and Paul had to spend the night in the hospital. The next day when he came home, Mother screamed, "You're no good for nothing — you're a pain in my ass!"

Mother would run around the house chasing Jeremy with the broom and hitting him as hard as she could. She would chase him down to the basement and then lock the door behind him. Jeremy got out through a small window — it was a tight fit, but he made it out safety. Jeremy called a friend to pick him up.

Such abuse went on until my parents divorce in 1980, when Mother kicked Paul out of the house for good. He was only fourteen years old.

CHAPTER FIVE

MOVING OUT

When Mother threw Paul out of the house, Dad called our older sister Susan. Dad wanted to get Paul away from Mother before something terrible happened. So Paul went to live with Susan in Hayward, California when he was fourteen years old. He enrolled at a local school and got a job as a newspaper boy so he could earn some money of his own. It was not much but — at least it was something.

Susan helped Paul get his first paper route. She also helped him get his drivers license when he was sixteen years old. She took him fishing and they did a lot of outdoor activities. Susan and Paul baked cookies and prepared meals together and had tremendous fun doing it.

Paul took Driver's Education; he loved cars and knew all their ins and outs. He stayed with Susan until he was sixteen years old, and then moved on. For a while he lived with brother Dennis in Santa Clara. But Paul was too much for Dennis to handle, so again he had to move on. Paul next lived with brother Philip, but Philip had more responsibilities than he could handle. So finally Paul called me. This was quite a surprise, as I was living in Oregon at the time.

He said, "Peggy I want to move in with you." I thought he was joking; but the next day, I heard a knock at my front door. It was Paul. I was very surprised and said, "You weren't kidding about moving in!"

Paul had just earned his drivers license and made the eight-hour drive from San Jose, California to Bend, Oregon overnight. He drove a white 1960 LeSaber station wagon, which was in pretty good shape for such an old car. Paul took very good care of that car; he changed the oil, tuned up the engine, and bled the brakes. He also tuned up my car.

* * *

We had a lot of great times together. We waited in line for hours to see movie like *E. T.* and *Blue Lagoon*. Paul loved living with my family. He started taking acting classed at the town theater in Bend, Oregon that year.

Then I had a call from my sister Susan, who also needed a place to live. So she moved in too. At first, it was really nice having both my brother and sister living with my family. But then one day Paul and Susan got into a big fight, with a lot of fist-hitting, slapping and screaming. I think Paul was jealous of Susan living with me.

Paul punched Susan in the eye! — He was in trouble now. Susan's eye was badly-swollen and didn't look good. The next day, Paul began acting mean to everyone. Susan left and moved in with a friend. We did not hear from her for a long time after that.

Then one day, Paul was playing with one of my daughters. Jeanette was eleven years old at the time. Paul was pretending to slap Jeanette across the face. She was wearing braces. When I saw Jeanette's face bleeding, I was furious. "What the hell is the matter with you? Why did you do that?" I was so mad that I told him he had to leave.

I did not mean it literally, but Paul took it that way.

My brother moved out. He was gone. I was very upset not knowing where he was. Later in the day, I received phone call from Paul. "I'm living at a friend's house now," he said. "Don't worry about me — I'm okay."

I wondered whether he was really okay — or was he just saying that so I wouldn't worry?

CHAPTER SIX

PAUL BECOMES JEREMY

The next day I met Paul at his friend's house. We had lunch together at a shopping mall and saw a movie. Then it was getting late and I had to pick up my kids from school. I saw Paul a few more times that year. Finally I heard from one of my sisters that he had moved away.

Rosemary said that when she mailed Paul a Christmas card that year, she put her address and phone number inside. He called and thanked her for the card. That was the last time she heard from him. Paul called other relatives and asked if he could stay with them because he had no place to go. Nobody said yes. None of use ever heard from Paul after that ...

* * *

I learned later that my brother changed his name from Paul Andrew Boyce to Jeremy Elliott Applegate at the Deschutes County Courthouse in Oregon on September 1, 1983. He took his middle name from the character Elliott in the movie *E. T.*

Paul called Dad and asked if he should try acting. Dad said, "Sure, give it a try." That was the last time Dad talked to my brother. No one in our family heard from Paul ever again. It seemed he had disappeared of the face of the Earth — didn't stay in contact with any of his family or friends.

Then in 1988, I was watching a Movie of the Week one night on television. It was called *Scandal,* starred Rachel Welsh, and was set in a small town. I like Rachel Welsh so I watched it.

Half-an-hour into the movie, I saw my brother Paul playing a high-school student talking to Rachel Welsh's daughter.

I could not believe my eyes. I turned on the VCR and I taped the show. I was so excited and happy for him that he was making it as an actor.

CHAPTER SEVEN

AN ACTOR AT LAST

Over the years, Jeremy Applegate had parts in a few motion pictures. Throughout the 1980's, he had numerous guest star and recurring roles on television shows like *My Two Dad's, Our House,* and 21 *Jump Street.* He appeared in *Heathers* (1989) as Peter Dawson. In 1994, he was in the television movie *Lies of the Heart: The Story of Laurie Kellogg.* Jeremy was also in *Strange Teen* (1996) and *The Cable Guy (*1996*).* He also appeared in a few commercials for Long John Silvers. After that, we didn't see him on television or in any movies.

* * *

OVER THE YEARS THAT HAVE PASSED SINCE THEN, WE HAVE HEARD FROM A NUMBER OF MY BROTHER'S FRIENDS. THE FOLLOWING INFORMATION IS BASED ON WHAT THEY TOLD US:

Kim Giles wrote to me about the years my brother was missing, and I got information from letters Jeremy wrote to her. She helped fill in some of the blanks.

Jeremy Applegate made-up a fictitious background for his early life. He told people that he was born May 10, 1968 in Texas ... That his real parents were very rich and were killed in airplane crash when he was very young ... That after his parents' death, he was left in an orphanage ... That he ran away to Hollywood to become an actor.

Kim told me that Jeremy liked to work on cars. He had a BMW and he could fix and knew every part on his car. He was a whiz on the computer. He had a nose job in 1997 because he had a lot of trouble breathing and his noise was too wide on the sides.

He lived in twenty-four different places since first arriving in Los Angeles in 1984. He didn't have the energy or the inclination to find anywhere else to live.

Jeremy had degenerative disk disorder in his neck that was the result of a motorcycle accident . Jeremy tried acupuncture. The doctor put eleven needles in the lump in his neck — and it really worked so that he could go on casting interviews.

When facing adversity, Jeremy would fight to the end — but whenever he lost, he would say, "I'm going to kill myself." He was frequently suicidal and seeing a psychiatrist. He was taking Xanax as well as many other prescription drugs. He was in and out of mental hospitals all of his adult life.

* * *

Jeremy had two cats — named Clarice and Febe. He loved his cats, and they provided the only affection he ever got. Jeremy named his cat Clarice after Clarice Starling in *Silence of the Lambs*. The other cat, Febe, was one of Clarice's babies.

The only things Jeremy really liked was watching *South Park* and *Star Trek* on television. He was definitely a Trekkie — and even had his own Starfleet uniform. He liked Buddy Holly, Chinese food, Italian food, and coffee. He did not drink alcohol but smoked marijuana every day around 4:00 PM. Jeremy had a 2002 BMW which he converted into a 1969 model. He liked working on it and making it go fast.

He was always very unhappy and frequently suicidal. I read in some of his letters that he would put his gun in his mouth, unlock the trigger — then do some hard thinking then take it out. He hated himself. He smoked a lot of pot.

Jeremy would sleep throughout the daytime hours. He frequently missed rehearsals or job interviews because of his depression. The medications would work for a while — but then he would smoke too much pot. He took diet pills and he would stay up all night. He loved to drive fast — and had too many traffic speeding tickets. He did not like people of any kind of authority.

* * *

Jeremy evidently had the same mental illness that runs in my family. He was so paranoid that he would sleep with a loaded shotgun. Jeremy hated anyone who caused him any pain.

CHAPTER EIGHT

PROBLEMS

Jeremy had arguments with his next-door neighbor, a man named Singh, who claimed that Jeremy had parked in his parking space. Singh left two nasty notes threatening Jeremy if he parked there again. When Jeremy tried to reason with Singh, the man started screaming in his face, becoming increasingly violent. So Jeremy took out a canister of tear gas as a precaution. Singh saw this and tried to force his way into Jeremy's apartment. Jeremy chased him off with the tear gas.

The next day when Jeremy went out to the mailbox, this neighbor started to provoke him again. Jeremy took out his tear gas, so Singh ran inside and dialed 911. Then Singh told my brother "Don't go anywhere — they are coming for you!" Two police squad cars showed up and Singh told them that Jeremy had threatened him for no reason. He went on ranting about the parking space. The police realized that Singh was a psycho and told Jeremy, "If he gets out of control again, give him a good dose of that tear gas."

My brother wrote a letter to his landlord about this neighbor, after which Singh changed completely and began asking Jeremy to drive him around to get or parts for his car. It was bizarre.

* * *

Jeremy called his doctor's office for a refill on his medication, stating that he was suicidal and wanted to talk with the doctor. The nurse refused; he called her a bitch and she hung up. The nurse told the answering service not to take any messages from Jeremy. He finally got hold of the doctor and explained to him what was going on. About a week later, Jeremy received a certified letter from his doctor stating that he would no longer treat Jeremy. No explanation was given, and Jeremy's phone calls were never returned.

* * *

Jeremy had problems with his landlord, Mr. Chin. The man put notes on Jeremy's car saying that the car was abandoned. Which was not the case ... He put a warning card on Jeremy's BMW to move it every 72 hours or the car would be picked up. When a meter maid came and impounded the car, Jeremy had to pay a $160.oo fine.

Mr. Chin hadn't change the locks on the apartment when Jeremy moved in. Jeremy didn't complain — he was just relieved to have a roof over his head. So he took it upon himself to purchase new locks and install them. About a week after that, he lost his keys. He thought they were probably lost in the mess of his room. Therefore, he re-keyed the locks to save Chin money and took it off his rent. When he called the property owner and told him about the new locks, Chin came very upset.

So Jeremy paid the rent for that month — but the very next day, Chin slipped the check back under the door. Jeremy called to find out what the problem was and left numerous messages —

but received no return calls. On May11, 1998 the landlord gave Jeremy a 3-day notice to pay or quit. This was also slipped under the door. It didn't make sense because Jeremy had paid and the landlord returned the money. Then on May 26, Jeremy was served with eviction papers that said he had five days to respond or the sheriff would remove him forcibly.

All this affected Jeremy very badly, making him more suicidal, depressed, and unable to sleep. He was vomiting, running a 102-degree temperature, and had high blood pressure. Jeremy tried to get his allergy shots but his blood pressure was too high. The allergy nurse was worried about him; it was nice that Jeremy had someone who cared what happened to him.

Jeremy had a lot of worries. He tried to get legal advice, but the low-income programs were shut down. His medical problems were erratic. He would feel okay one day — then his mood would change and he'd hate himself as well as anyone who'd ever hurt him. He slept all day, missed two calls from his agent, and then went back to sleep depressed again. He hated his life, having to hang on all day and then doing it all over again the next day.

Life really was bad for Jeremy. He called his friends and told them he was going to end it all. They thought he was just crying wolf — but in reality, he was crying for help. If only someone had checked his background and found out where he really came from ... maybe we could have found him and helped.

Jeremy just wanted a place to call his own and to have good friends he could count on. However, that never happened for him. Jeremy he had to fight for life from the very beginning to the bitter end — and the struggle eventually killed him.

He stood up for what he thought was right. He was very intelligent. He knew just the right people to talk to and how to get results. All Jeremy wanted was a normal life — but in his own view, he was an only child orphaned at a very young age.

Jeremy had many problems with people in positions of authority. He could not and would not take orders from anyone, largely because he was bipolar — manic depressive — as well as schizophrenic. When Jeremy was suicidal, he would take the trigger-lock off his shot gun and put the barrel into his mouth.

He was terrified with nightmares. This may have been a side effect to the Mirtazapine medication he was on. He wished that the Grays from UFOs would take him away so he wouldn't have to follow rules ever again. He talked about space aliens and believed they were real.

Jeremy never told any of his friends the true story of his life and family. If only he had contacted one of us — we would have tried to help. He needed his family, but his doctors thought that would be a big mistake. The doctors over-medicated him. The last mental hospital where Jeremy was last treated was in Pasadena — a hospital well-known to the Hollywood stars — but which has had hundreds of complaints on how they handle patients there.

Jeremy just wanted the pain to go away. It was Christmas, and he hated spending holidays alone. He thought it out carefully this time. He was going to end the pain, he could not go on any more.

He made one final call to a friend to say that he was going to end it all. His friend called the police and told them what was going on. The police phoned Jeremy — but he didn't care anymore. He had his made up his mind that life was not worth living. Jeremy Applegate put the shot gun in his mouth pulled back the trigger-lock as he had done so many times before.

CHAPTER NINE

SUICIDE

At 1835 hours on 23 March, 2000, police officers received a phone call from a friend of Jeremy's and dispatched squad cars and a SWAT team. Upon arrival at his apartment, they made telephone contact with Jeremy and spent a considerable of amount of time on the phone attempting to dissuade him from killing himself. At 2115 hours, a Supervisor took the phone and was just beginning to speak when officers heard a loud report sound from the apartment. The SWAT team shot tear gas into the apartment and forced entry through the apartment door ...

The building was situated on a hill on the West side of Hillcrest Avenue south of Braham. The location was a multi-unit apartment with access to each by means of an outside staircase. The entrance opened up into a living room/bedroom combination. There was a single bed placed in the southwest corner of the living room. There were dishes and newspapers everywhere. As if he did not clean up because he simply did not care anymore.

They found the descendent inside with a gunshot wound to the head. Paramedics were summoned to the scene and pronounced Jeremy dead at 2350 hours. One officer made numerous calls to names and numbers found in his address book in an attempt to trace the family of the decedent.

One friend the police contacted said Jeremy had been threatening suicide for years that he'd always said that he was going to shoot himself with his shotgun. He said Jeremy had been worried about a pending court date for a DUI arrest in Ventura County. He'd told the friend that his parents were dead — as results of either a plane crash or auto crash. The story of his parent's death was never consistent.

The police called Jeremy's conservator, Kim Giles — but she was not home at the time. They left a message. When Kim returned from an out-of-town trip, she got the message and rushed over to Jeremy's apartment; but the police would not let her go inside or touch anything.

Kim knew there were family members somewhere, but she never looked for or contacted anyone. Her name was listed as conservator on all Jeremy's legal papers as well as on his bank account. She had my brother cremated and his ashes scattered at sea in May of 2000.

* * *

We learned of my brother's death when Mother died and Aunt Nancy did an online search so that we could notify Paul. Instead, we found his death notice. I sent for his death certificate and told my other siblings that Paul was dead. No one could believe it.

His former roommate made a Memory Book for us — that's all we have left of my brother. Old letters, some photo's, a few records ...

Not a day goes by that I don't think about my beloved brother. He was only 34 years old — way too young to die. But he will never be forgotten. May he rest in peace ...

Angels with silver wings
Shouldn't know suffering.
I wish I could take the pain for you.

If God has a master plan,
Then only he understands.
I hope it's your eyes he's seeing through.

~P2~

CHAPTER TEN

FILMOGRAPHY

The Cable Guy (1996) (uncredited) — played Serf #4

The Story: It's a time-honored urban ritual: Slip the cable guy fifty bucks and you'll get all the movie channels for free. But when Steven Kovacs moves into a new apartment, his Cable Guy is not like the others. He doesn't want your fifty bucks; all he wants is a friend ... and he won't take no for an answer. Steven is about to learn that there's no such thing as free cable.

Jeremy Applegate plays a medieval serf.

Jeremy is wearing a green medieval times outfit and is on "Matthew Broderick's team," He dresses Matthew Broderick in his battle gear and is seen dragging him away when he falls. Jeremy is only in the medieval times scenes.

Lies of the Heart: The Story of Laurie Kellogg (1994) (TV) — played Strange Teen

Lies of the Heart: The Story of Laurie Kellogg

Filmed in Los Angeles by MDT Productions and Daniel H. Blatt Productions in association with Warner Brothers Television. Executive producers, Daniel H. Blatt, Judith Paige Mitchell; producer, Sam Manners; director, Michael Uno; writer, Mitchell.

Cast: Jennie Garth, Gregory Harrison, Steven Keats, Francis Guinan, T.C. Warner, Robin Frates, Alexis Arquette, Sharon Spelman, Jeff Doucette, Virginya Keehne, Gina Phillips, Phil Buckman, William Wellman Jr., Robert Cavanaugh, Robert Factor, Heather Lauren Olsen, Mitchell Binder, Ben Block, Douglas Roberts , William Hubbard Knight, Suzanne Dean, Jeremy Applegate, Sara Moonves, Stephanie Sawyer, Elan Rothschild, Melissa Hunter, Haley Osment, Alexander Lester.

Proving there's life beyond "90210," Jenny Garth tackles the tough role of a young bride who, after suffering years of abuse at the hands of her older husband, Bruce (Gregory Harrison), snaps and encourages her teenage friends to murder him. Based on a true story, "Lies" occasionally suffers from low production qualities, but the horrific tales of abuse and the sordid mess that was her marriage are transmitted with great emotional depth.

The telepic starts with Laurie awaiting trial and looking back at the events, aided by an occasional narration. Each prison scene begins in slo-mo with a blue , grainy screen adding to the character looking back in wonderment at how her life has turned out.

The story, spanning ten years, begins with 16-year-old Laurie meeting Bruce in a bar, and as their relationship develops, so does Bruce's obsession with younger women (it is hinted that he was playing more than hide-and-seek with some of the neighborhood kids that Laurie baby-sat).

It is well established early on that Laurie is a sympathetic character who is naive about life, is devoted to her husband and will stop at nothing to please him.

He takes terrifying advantage of this; Bruce seems nice but his abusive interior begins to surface little by little until he becomes a monster: beating her, abusing her mentally, and threatening to kill her and their children. The changes in his psyche are realistically developed over a period of time.

Garth does well with the role, suffering only in the far-from-believable, hasty scenes where she is interviewed by reporters on the way to court. Garth is good at the initial teenage innocence required for the role, but there is very little change in her appearance over a period of ten years. Surely someone in makeup could have helped.

Acting .Jeremy plays one of the strange teens helping Laurie Kellogg with the death of her husband. (A very small part)

"Lies" carries a warning — as it should — that the abuse portrayed is shocking, not always from the visually graphic, but from what is hinted at and described.

Hard Copy — "Too Young to Love" (1993) TV Episode — played Mark Sotka

Jeremy plays a very abusive boy in this movies. He forces him self on the young woman, he takes control of situation then everything gets out of control. A very good part for Jeremy.

Davis Rules – "The Moment of Youth" (1992) TV Episode — played Mel

Jeremy plays one of the children, as Mel in one episode.(a guest on the show only one episode)

Dwight Davis, a widower and grammar school principal, has the task of raising his three sons, along with the help of his wacky father Gunny. After the series moved from ABC to CBS, the oldest son and his friend were dropped and Dwight's sister was added. Added as well was Skinner, a son of some of Dwight's college pals who moved in. It was explained Skinner's parents were archaeologists located in Latin America. Also the oldest son was said to have become a foreign exchange student. Appearing occasionally was Dwight's love interest Erika, but she soon ran off and joined a convent.

5. Heathers (1989) — played Peter Dawson

Jeremy Applegate plays Peter Dawson, a student body president handing out papers on teenage suicide.

Veronica mingles with Heather I, II and III to be as popular as them, even though she hates them. She hates them enough to wish they were dead, but she would never want to be their cause of death though. When she starts dating Jason Dean, however, she finds herself involved in the murdering of most of her enemies, covered up as suicides.

Three high school girls named Heather run an iron clad social clique at high school. One of their anointees, Veronica, isn't sure she wants to fit into the clique, particularly when she has to snub some of her old friends at the Heathers' behest. When Veronica meets the new guy at school, she starts pulling away from the clique, while some of the more popular students start showing up dead with suicide notes.

Dear Diary: Veronica Sawyer is sick of being part of the Heathers, the most powerful clic of Westerberg High; making fun of Martha Dunnstock ("Dumptruck"), the fat girl, or doing some stupid polls is something she'll never get used to. Meanwhile she meets JD, a cool rebel guy who wouldn't mind shooting a gun at school just to make his point. Remington University's party is where Veronica has to go as a Heather, and there's where she gets her ultimatum as a Heather from Heather Chandler, the head of the Heathers. So Veronica and her lover JD "accidentally" kill Heather Chandler and manage to cover it up by making a suicide note. Will this be just the beginning of the assasination-turned-suicide serie of Westerberg High which nor the FBI, the CIA or the PTA would be able to stop? Or will Veronica be able to pull herself together and stop her psychotic lover from killing absolutely EVERYONE at school?

6. Scandal in a Small Town (1988) — played Kid

Jeremy plays a student at the high school. It was a speaking part; Jeremy's line was: "Julie, how many Jews does it take to screw in a light bulb?"

7. Our House – "Out of Step" (1988) TV Episode — played Eric

The Series: Following the death of his son, Gus Witherspoon takes in his daughter-in-law and his three grandchildren to live with him. Adjustment to the new arrangement is not easy on any of them.

The Episode: Kris Witherspoon is upset over an editorial about her candidacy for student council in the student paper that her mother serves as advisor for. Jeremy Applegate plays Eric.

Eric writes a story making fun of the candidates including Kris, Jessie thinks the article (satire) is good and tells Kris she is going to run it in the student paper. This was a great part for Jeremy to play. It was like him in real life.Jeremy loved acting and was great he put his heart and soul in every part he played.

Superior Court – "Yes, Mother" (1987) TV Episode — played Dean Ogden

Jeremy plays Dean Ogden as one of the children(a small part as an extra).

On the heels of the successful "Divorce Court," "Superior Court" was among a wave of reality-based courtroom dramas released in the late 1980s. Both criminal and civil procedings were presented, with most cases involving shock value rather than routine cases. Examples of cases included a defendant tried for murdering another man, but the defendant claimed he saw the actual perpetrator in a dream; and a man who sued a financial institution after a banker swindled him out of $10 million.

PHOTO ALBUM

Paul with a cat at the age of two years old.

Paul playing Hide-and-Go-Seek in the fireplace.

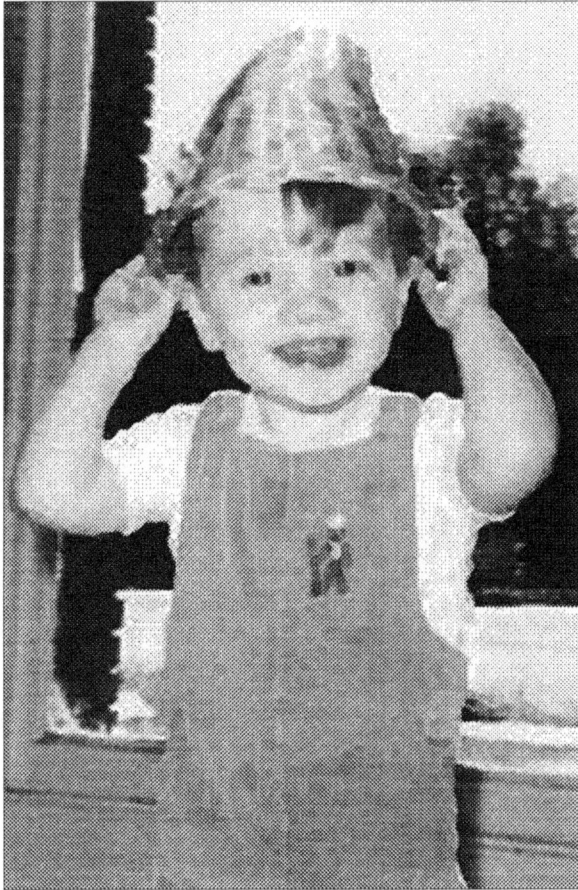

Paul at the age of three years old.

Paul as a Ring Bearer in sister Rosemary's wedding.

Rosemary's wedding in 1973.

Paul in Kindergarden at Trace Elementy in 1970.

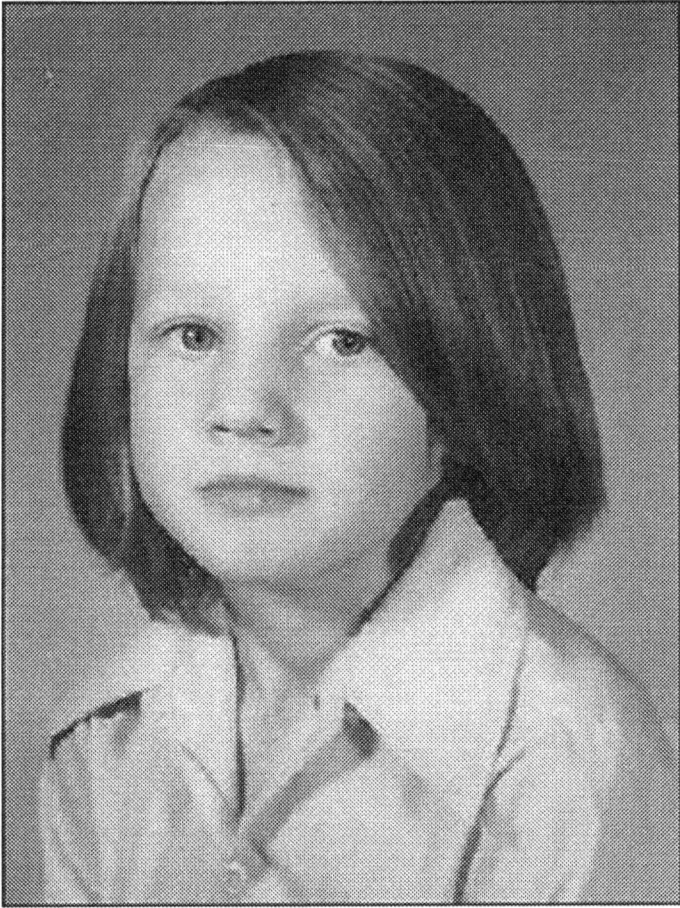

Paul in 1st Grade at Trace Eelementry in 1971.

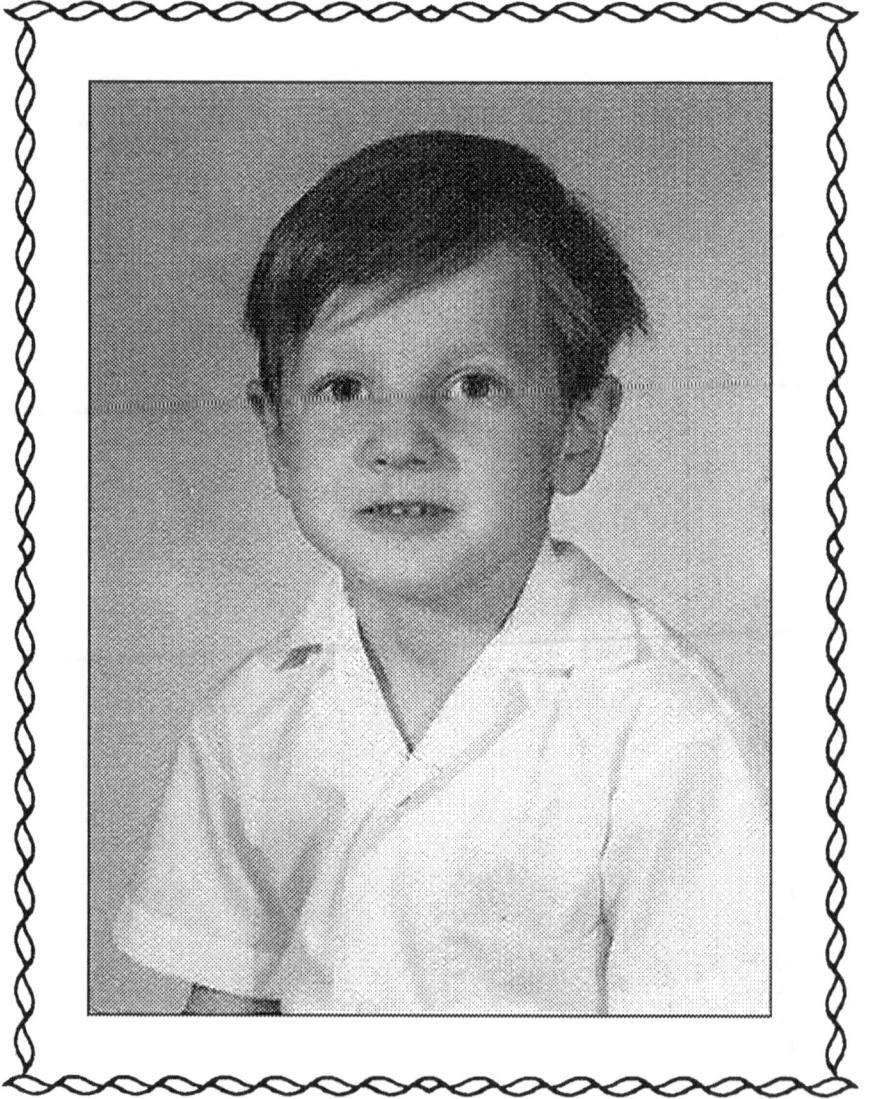

Paul in 2nd Grade at Trace Elementry in 1972.

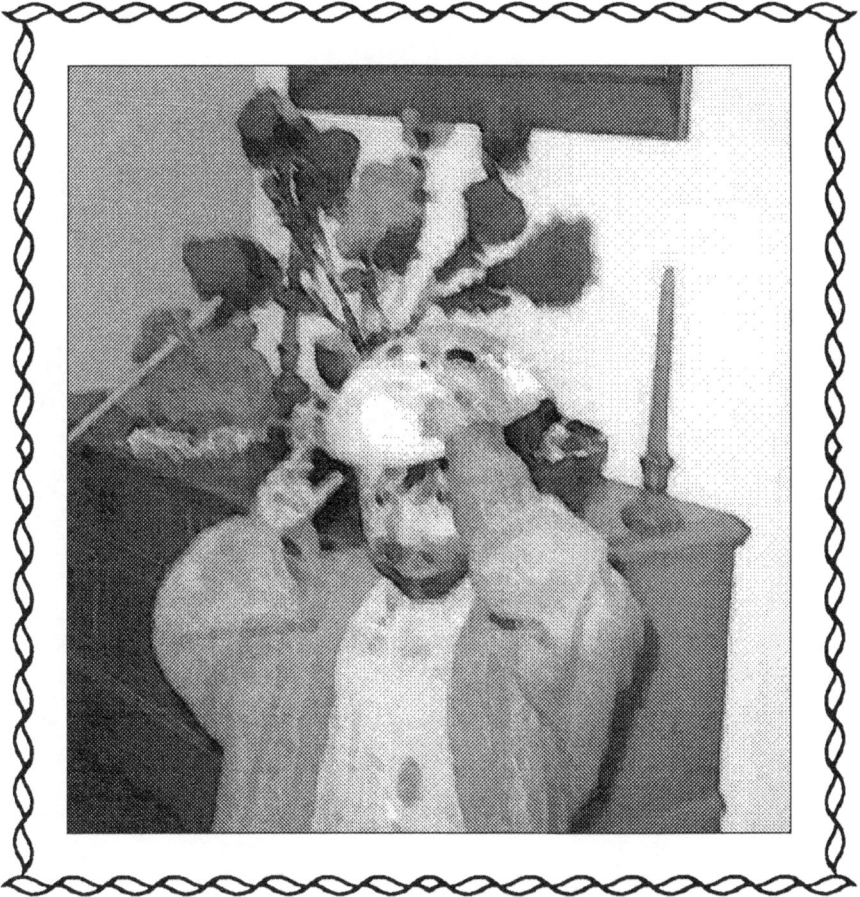

Paul at Holloween dressed as a hobo.

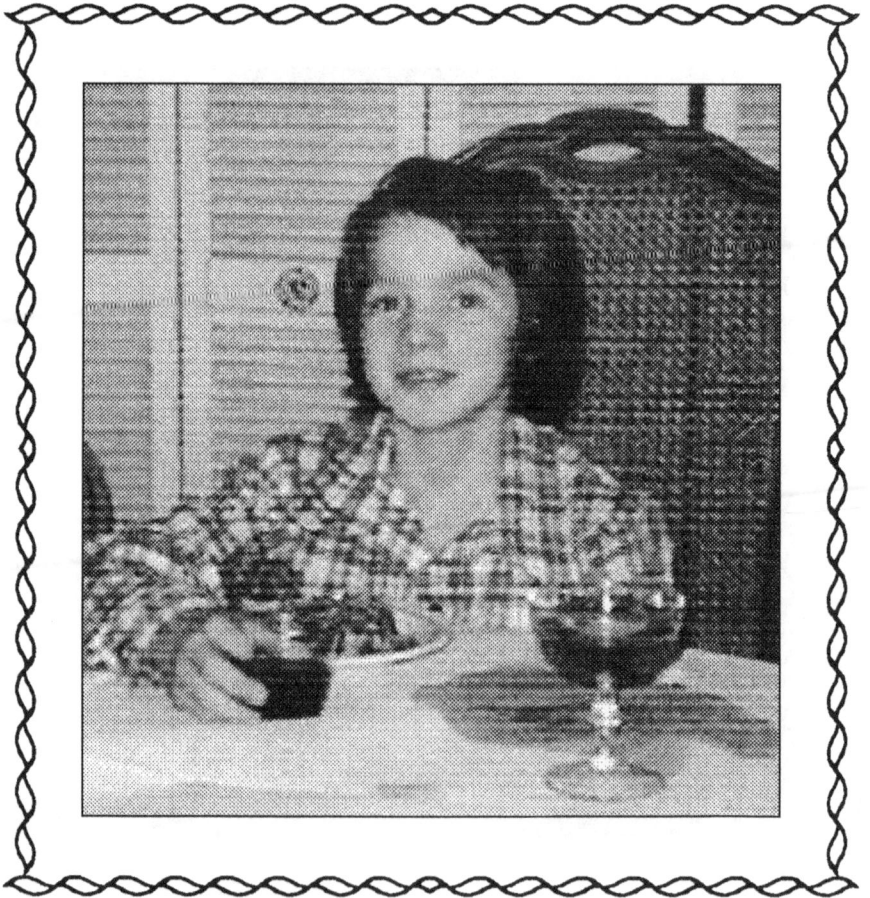

Paul having dinner at sister Marian's house.

Looking over family album with sister Susan and Dad at home.

Paul in 4th Grade.

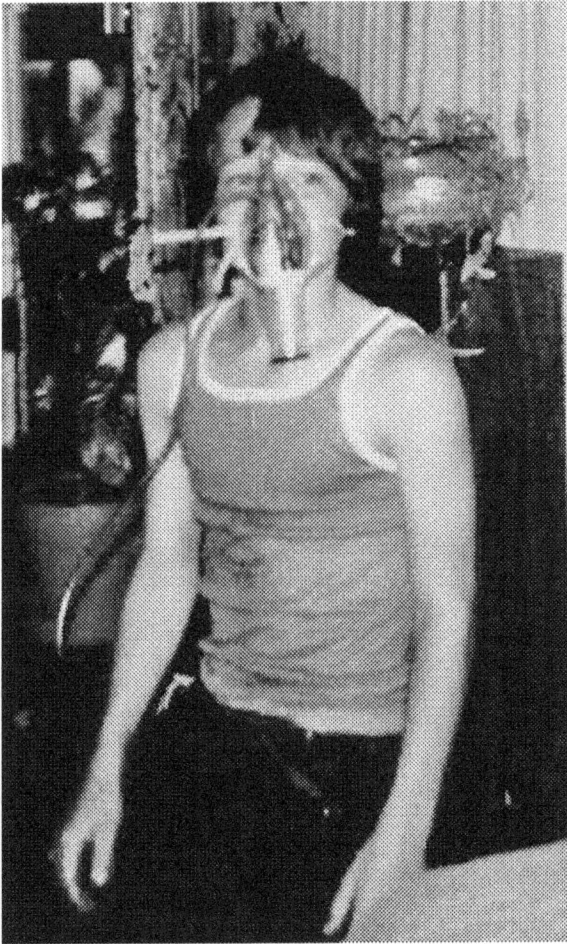

Paul using his nebulizer machine posing as Darth Vador.

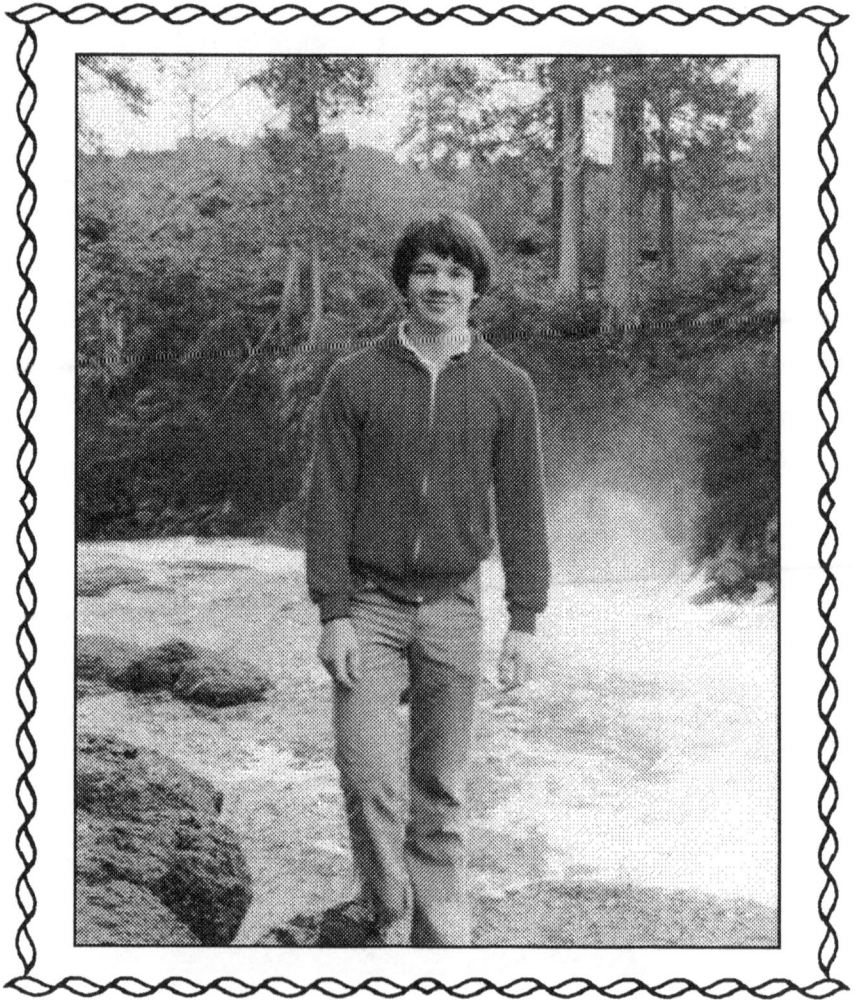

Paul at Deshutes River Bend, Oregon.

EULOGIES

Jeremy

For Paul's Family:

It's always hard loosing a loved one, even more so in this way. You will always be in my thoughts and prayers. God Bless.

— *Anonymous*

⤜∾⤏

For Jeremy:

Heathers is my favorite film, you were such a talented actor. I only wish I could have seen you in more films.

Much love,

— *TWY*

⤜∾⤏

It is the hope of all we might have been that fills me with the hope to wish impossible things.

— *P2*

I think about you everyday Jeremy, and I will forever.

> I hear the wind call your name
> It calls me back home again
> It sparks up the fire
> A flame that still burns ...

I love you and I miss you so much.

— Angie

You were a good friend. I thought you were a riot on the set. You taught me how to keep it from getting boring. You are missed. Peace be with you.

— Joe

Rest in peace. I'm sorry you took your life. You were a great actor. I love *21 Jump Street* and I heard they're making it into a movie. You are not Forgotten. CYA in Heaven.

— Daredevil

Young man, you were such a beloved actor. I'm sorry you thought there was no other way. Rest in Peace. See you in Heaven.

— Mary

Jeremy, my brother — I miss celebrating all the holidays together, especially making Christmas ornaments for the tree. I miss all the fun times we had, working on cars, all the great restaurants, laughing ... I wish I'd been a bigger part of your life.

I remember the last picture I took of you standing on a rock next to the Dechutes River. I remember the day you signed up at the Bend Theater to be in a play — that was the beginning of your acting career. I remember you once asking me about the name Jeremy Elliott Applegate. I said it was a nice name, but didn't think anything more of it. I didn't know till much later that was to be your stage name. I wish I could somehow fill in all those years we missed being together. You will always be in our hearts. I love you, my dear brother Jeremy.

I miss you brother, and wish you were here celebrating Christmas with your family. I think about you every day — if only I could have been there for you.

— Peggy